# The Essential Book of Awesome Jokes for 7-9 year Old Kids

## Hilarious Jokes, Ridiculous Facts and Tongue Twisters that make you Laugh Out Loud

Dave P. Williams

# Table of Contents

# Introduction

Hi! Welcome to The Essential Book of Awesome Jokes for Kids! In your hands, you hold one of the funniest books you'll ever come across. That's a promise! We've compiled some of the best knock-knock jokes, one-liners, riddles, tongue-twisters, and ridiculously-funny facts for you to laugh your lungs out too.

We've structured this book in an easy to read way: the jokes have been divided into sections, so if you're looking for a specific kind of joke, simply flip your way to that section. It's that easy! There are hundreds and hundreds of jokes in this book, so try to read them all.

With this book in your hands, you're going to be the funniest kid on the block. Crack a few of these at your next birthday party, or on the playground, and you're sure to have everyone cackling within minutes.

This is the class clown's handbook. And if you aren't the class clown, you soon will be!

**WARNING: This book is guaranteed to make you laugh your hardest, so if you aren't ready to shed some tears of laughter, then stop reading here!**

# Hilarious Jokes

We're starting off strong in this chapter. In it, there are hundreds of one-liners, tongue-twisters, and ridiculous facts. Be prepared to laugh your guts out for the next few pages, because they are packed with some of the funniest jokes you'll ever hear.

Ready? Let's get right into the laughter!

# One-Liners

The first Apple computer was used by Adam and Eve, and it only had one byte of memory. Everything crashed from there.

I would tell you a chemistry joke, but I know I wouldn't get a reaction.

At first, I wasn't going to get a brain transplant, but then I changed my mind.

Everyone my age is older than me...

Did you hear about the man who was hit with a can of soda? He was lucky it was a soft drink.

I got a new pair of gloves yesterday, but both of them are 'lefts', which, on one hand, is great, but on the other, it's just not right.

I used to think I couldn't make up my mind, but now I'm not really sure...

Don't spell part backwards. It's a trap.

You shouldn't trust atoms. They make up everything.

Rest in peace, boiled water. You will be mist.

The past, the present, and the future walked into a room. Things got a little tense.

I just found out that I'm colorblind. The diagnosis came totally out of the green.

I used to be addicted to the hokey pokey, but I was able to turn myself around.

Did Noah bring termites onto the Ark?

Don't you get annoyed when someone answers their own questions? I do.

I hate it when people use big words to make themselves look indecisive.

True friendship is walking into your friend's house and having your phone connect to the WiFi automatically.

My dad bought a vacuum a few months ago, and all it does is gather dust.

Yesterday, my friend was complaining that I never listen to him, or something like that...

Maybe if we tell people the brain is an app, they'll start using it.

You might fall from a ladder, you might fall from a tree, but the best place to fall... is in love with me!

My mom's email password was hacked. That's the fourth time we've had to rename the cat.

People who eat snails probably don't like fast food.

To the mathematicians who came up with the number zero: Thanks for nothing!

What's the best part of living in Switzerland? Well, the flag is a big plus.

I eat my tacos over another tortilla. That way, when the stuff falls out, BOOM, another taco.

The conclusion is the part where you got bored of thinking.

Becoming a vegetarian was a big missed steak.

Never trust a dog to watch your food.

Of course, I can keep secrets, but the people I tell them to can't.

I could really see myself cleaning mirrors.

Spoiler alert! The milk has been in the fridge for three weeks.

If I refuse to take a nap, am I resisting a rest?

It's impossible to annoy me with bird puns because toucan play at that game.

If at first, you don't succeed, we have a lot in common.

My dad is a road worker, and I didn't want to believe that he was stealing from his job, but the signs were all there when I got home.

Two fish are in a tank. The one asks the other, "Hey, how do you drive this thing?"

My dad likes to wash the car with me. I wish he would use a sponge instead.

I wrote a song about tortillas. Well, it's more of a rap.

A short psychic escaped from jail. Now there's a short medium at large.

Yesterday, I found a rock that was 1 760 yards long. That has to be some sort of milestone.

My teacher told me to have a good day, so I went home.

Did you hear about the kidnapping that happened at school? Don't worry; he woke up.

My math teacher called me average. How mean.

I would make a sodium joke, but Na…

My teacher asked me if I was ignorant or just apathetic. I told her that I don't know, and I don't care.

Why did the students eat their homework? Because the teacher said it was a piece of cake.

You're like school during summer. No class.

The M&M went to school because she really wanted to be a Smartie.

I'm really thankful to my teacher, who taught the word 'many' to me. It means a lot.

We're going on a field trip to the Coca-Cola factory. I hope there isn't a pop quiz.

Why didn't the skeleton go to prom? He had nobody to dance with.

My mom got me a book on procrastination at the start of the year. I'll open it tomorrow.

I can't count how many times I've failed math.

Keep your dream alive by hitting the snooze button.

You aren't fat; you're just easier to see.

How do you make a waterbed bouncier? Use spring water.

Always give 100%, no matter what you do. Unless you're donating blood.

First day of my new diet, I removed all fattening foods from the fridge. It was delicious.

There are three types of people in the world: those that can count, and those that can't.

When I first got a universal remote, I thought, "this changes everything!"

I was addicted to soap, but I'm clean now.

I'm on a seafood diet. I see food, and I eat it.

I dressed up as an almond for Halloween. Everyone thought I was nuts.

Writing with a broken pencil is pointless.

The World Tongue-Twister Champion was just arrested. He's probably going to get a tough sentence.

Take my advice. I'm not using it.

Dogs have owners. Cats have staff.

As a wizard, I like to turn things into glass. Just wanted to make that clear.

With great reflexes comes great response ability.

My IQ test came back negative.

My bike wouldn't stand up by itself. I guess it was two tired.

Escalators don't malfunction; they just turn into stairs.

I hate peer pressure, and so should you.

I think it's weird that people get attacked by sharks. Don't they hear the music?

What did the one eye say to the other eye? "Something smells between us."

I tried to escape the Apple store, but I couldn't because there were no Windows.

Seagulls fly over the sea because if they flew over the bay, they'd be bagels.

Last time I stole a calendar, I got twelve months.

Are you made from copper and tellurium, because you're CuTe?

What do elves learn at school? The Elf-abet.

What kind of exam does a vampire teacher give his students? A blood test.

What did E.T's mom say when he got home? "Where on Earth have you been?"

My parents always tell me that their world does not revolve around me. That must mean I'm not their sun.

What do you call a priest that becomes a lawyer? A father in law.

I told my family I wanted to be a comedian, and all they did was laugh.

Dolphins are so smart that it only takes them a few weeks in captivity to train the humans to stand at the edge of the water and throw them fish.

My shin is a great tool for finding furniture in a dark room.

I'm planning on living forever. So far, so good.

Change is inevitable, just not from the vending machine.

Did Noah really have to bring mosquitoes onto the Ark?

It's amazing that all the news that happens in one day can fit into a single newspaper.

What color does a Smurf turn when it's choking?

I don't have an attitude. I just have a personality that's difficult to handle.

The Miss Universe pageant is rigged. All of the winners are from Earth!

The difference between fiction and reality is that fiction has to make sense.

What if there were no more hypothetical questions?

I'm actually quite humble for how great I am.

Celebrities work hard for their whole lives to become known, then cover up their faces with dark glasses to avoid being recognized.

If olive oil comes from olives, and corn oil comes from corn, then where does baby oil come from?

Everything is edible, but some things are only edible once in your life.

I'm going to get a map of the world to hang in my room. Then, I'm going to put a pin in all of the places I've been to. But first, I need to travel to the top two corners of the world, so that the map doesn't fall down.

Did you hear about the man that had his left arm and leg chopped off? He's all right now.

Without 'me', it's just 'aweso'.

If the number 2 pencil is the most popular kind, then why isn't it the number 1 pencil?

I stopped believing in Santa Claus, and now I get clothes for Christmas.

Two antennae met each other on a roof, fell in love, and got married. The wedding wasn't anything special, but the reception was fantastic.

Being superstitious causes bad luck.

Who decided to put an 's' in the word 'lisp'?

My best friends and I played hide and seek yesterday, but the game went on for hours! You know what they say: good friends are hard to find.

My teacher asked me to describe myself in four words. My answer was, "lazy..."

How did the ocean become friends with the beach? It kept on waving.

The other day, I heard about a mannequin that lost all of his friends. Apparently, it was because he's so clothes minded.

My mom bought a cat without telling the rest of the family yesterday. When my dad found out, he said, "You have to be kitten me!"

My dad wanted to open a bakery and pastry shop, but he didn't have enough dough.

How old should my dog be before I tell him he's adopted?

Letting the cat out of the bag is much, much easier than putting it back in.

Our dog is named 'Six Miles'. That way, every time my mom walks the dog, she can say that she walked Six Miles.

My mom told me to stop pretending to be a flamingo, so I had to put my foot down.

Insect puns are the worst. They really bug me.

What do you call a cow that has no legs? Ground beef.

Why couldn't the leopard play hide and seek? Because he always gets spotted.

Why should you never play a card game with a big, spotted cat? Because it's probably a cheetah.

Can a kangaroo jump higher than a skyscraper? Of course, it can; a skyscraper can't jump.

What is the difference between a hippo and a zippo? One is really heavy, and the other one is a little lighter.

Why do elephants wear yellow socks? So they can hide upside down in a bowl of custard.

Walking on grass is so dangerous. It's full of blades!

Cinderella never makes it onto the soccer team because she's always running away from the ball.

What do you call a room with no walls? A mushroom.

A plane crashed in the jungle, and every single person on board died. Now there are only the married couples left.

The scarecrow won the Nobel Peace Prize because of its outstanding service in its field.

What's brown and sticky? A stick.

The shopkeeper sells his batteries for nothing. I guess you could say that they're free of charge.

When you're looking for something, it will always be in the last place you look, because you'll stop looking when you find it.

Our pet fish has no eyes, so we named him fsh.

What do you call a sleeping bull? A bulldozer.

What does a ghost call its mom and dad? Its transparents.

You never see any giraffes in elementary school, because they are all in high school.

What do you call an old snowman? Water.

If life gives you melons, you're probably dyslexic.

What was the most useful invention after the first telephone? The second telephone.

How do you know if an ant is a girl or a boy? They're all girls; otherwise, they would all be uncles.

So, is there an uncle histamine?

How many months have 28 days in them? All of them.

Where can you find an elephant? The same place you lost it.

What's the best way to talk to a giant? Use big words.

What starts with keys, and has three letters? A car.

Why do you never see hippos hiding in trees? Because they're so good at it.

The best liar you know is not the best liar, you know.

Why do birds fly? Because it's much faster than walking.

The farmer rode his horse into town. He felt it was too heavy to carry.

Elevator jokes are the best. They work on so many levels.

Which side of a cat has the most hair? The outside.

What did one flea say to the other? "Should we walk or catch a dog?"

What do you call a sleeping dinosaur? A dino-snore.

What kind of key is used to open a banana? A monkey.

What card game do crocodiles love to play? Snap.

What is the dumbest animal in the jungle? The penguin.

If a melon falls into a river, does that make it a watermelon?

What did the apple say to the banana? Nothing, fruit can't talk.

Why do tigers have stripes? So that they don't get spotted.

Scuba divers fall backward into the water because if they fell forward, they'd still be in the boat.

What do Kermit the Frog, Sonic the Hedgehog, and Alexander the Great have in common? A middle name.

The farmer started jumping on his potato crops because he really wanted to grow mashed potatoes.

What did the tuna fish say when she bumped into a concrete wall? "Dam!"

The only reason the dog did so well at school was because he was the teacher's pet.

What do you call a sheep with no legs? A cloud?

The math book was so sad. It had so many unsolved problems.

How do porcupines kiss? Carefully.

What did the triangle say to the sphere? "You're pointless."

Where can you find a dog with no legs? The same place as before.

Can February March? No, but April May.

Twister is a tornado's favorite game.

The difference between a newspaper and a fridge is that I've never tried to swat a fly with my fridge.

When a cow breaks the sound barrier, it goes COW-BOOM!

What sounds like a parrot, and is orange? A carrot.

Why did the child bring a tall ladder to school? He really wanted to go to high school.

What are the worst illnesses to have at the same time? Alzheimer's and diarrhea, because you're constantly running, but you have no idea where.

What do you get someone who has everything? A burglar alarm.

What kind of haircuts do bumblebees like to get? Buzzcuts.

You would think that goldfish wouldn't be so cheap.

Which letters are not in the alphabet? The ones at the post office.

Maybe if we gave chickens some chairs, they wouldn't have to sit on their eggs!

Frogs are always happy because they eat whatever bugs them.

What do you call a bear that doesn't have any teeth? A gummy bear.

What stays in one corner all its life, but can travel around the world? A stamp.

What do you call a dog that can tell the time? A watchdog.

What do you call a fly that has no wings? A walk.

What do you call a fly that has no wings and no legs? A look.

When the clock strikes 13, what time is it? Time to get a new clock.

What's black and white and red all over? The newspaper.

How long do the legs on a giraffe have to be? Long enough to touch the ground.

What's the hardest part of skydiving? The ground.

What do you get when you cross a rabbit with an insect? Bugs Bunny.

When the wheel was invented, it caused a revolution.

Where do people that have two broken legs go? As far as they can crawl.

Why did the dinosaur cross the road? Because they hadn't evolved into chickens yet.

What do you call a droid that takes the long way around? R2 detour.

Saturday and Sunday are the strongest. The rest are all weak days.

My teacher thinks our class is so bright. She wears sunglasses to school every day.

What do you call a parrot that passed away? A polygon.

A geologist's favorite concert is a rock concert.

Are there any Halloween creatures that are good at math? Not unless you Count Dracula.

What is at the center of the world? The letter 'R'.

What types of roads do ghosts prefer to use? Dead ends.

What did the large flower say to the small flower? "Hey, bud."

What do you call bears that have no ears? B.

Why do golfers like to wear two pairs of pants? In case they get a hole in one.

What happened when the man sued an airline for losing his luggage. He lost the case.

What do you call an alligator that's wearing a vest? An investigator.

Robots are so fearless because they have nerves of steel.

Spelling is a wizard's favorite school subject.

If someone rolls their eyes at you, be sure to roll them back. They'll need those to see.

What has four wheels and flies? A garbage truck.

What language does nobody speak? Sign language.

What is heavy forward, and not backward? Ton.

The Thesaurus is the dinosaur with the best vocabulary.

Hot is faster because you can always catch a cold.

What do you call a deer that has no eye? No eye deer

What do you call a deer that has no eyes and no legs? Still no eye deer.

# Knock-Knock Jokes

Knock, knock.
*Who's there?*
Canoe.
*Canoe who?*
Canoe let me in? I'm tired of knocking.

Knock, knock.
    *Who's there?*
Orange.
    *Orange who?*
Orange you going to let me in?

Knock, knock.
*Who's there?*
Needle.
*Needle who?*
Needle little money for the movies.

Knock, knock.
*Who's there?*
Harry.
Harry who?
*Harry up and let me in, it's cold!*

Knock, knock.
*Who's there?*
Avenue.
*Avenue who?*
Avenue let me in before?

Knock, knock.
*Who's there?*
A herd.
*A herd who?*
A herd you were home, so I came over.

Knock, knock.
*Who's there?*
Otto.
*Otto who?*
Otto know. I forgot.

Knock, knock.
*Who's there?*
Henrietta.
*Henrietta who?*
Henrietta worm that lived in his apple.

Knock, knock.
*Who's there?*
Adore.
*Adore who?*
Adore's in between us. Open it!

Knock, knock.
*Who's there?*
Apple.
*Apple who?*

Knock, knock.
*Who's there?*
Orange.
*Orange who?*
Orange you glad I didn't say Apple again?

Knock, knock.
*Who's there?*
A little old lady.
*A little old lady who?*
I never knew you could yodel!

Knock, knock.
*Who's there?*
Olive.
*Olive who?*
Olive you long time.

Knock, knock.
*Who's there?*
Kirtch.
*Kirtch who?*
Bless you!

Knock, knock.
*Who's there?*
Will you remember me in a minute?
*Yes.*
Will you remember me in a day?
*Yes.*

Will you remember me in a week?
*Yes.*
Knock, knock.
*Who's there?*
You didn't remember me!

Knock, knock.
*Who's there?*
Luke.
*Luke who?*
Luke through the keyhole and find out.

Knock, knock.
*Who's there?*
Ivan.
*Ivan who?*
Ivan you let me in, or I'm coming in through the window!

Knock, knock.
*Who's there?*
Freddy.
*Freddy who?*
Freddy or not, I'm coming in!

Knock, knock.
*Who's there?*
Who.
*Who who?*
Wait, are you an owl?

Knock, knock.
*Who's there?*
Scold.
*Scold who?*
Scold out here, let me in.

Knock, knock.
*Who's there?*
Police!
*Police who?*
Police let me in, I'm getting tired of knocking.

Knock, knock.
*Who's there?*
Ben.
*Ben who?*
Ben knocking for 15 minutes, let me in already.

Knock, knock.
*Who's there?*
Watson.
*Watson who?*
Watson TV today?

Knock, knock.
*Who's there?*
Spell.
*Spell who?*
W-H-O

Knock, knock.
*Who's there?*
Norma Lee.
*Norma Lee who?*
Norma Lee I don't have to knock so many times to get an answer!

Knock, knock.
*Who's there?*
CD.
*CD who?*
CD person at your door?

Knock, knock.
*Who's there?*
Somebody too short to ring the bell!

Knock, knock.
*Who's there?*
Nobel.
*Nobel who?*
Nobel, so I had to knock.

Knock, knock.
*Who's there?*
Tank.
*Tank who?*
My pleasure.

Knock, knock.
*Who's there?*
Figs.
*Figs who?*
Figs your doorbell, I hate knocking!

Knock, knock.
*Who's there?*
Cow says.
*Cow says who?*
No, cow goes moo!

Knock, knock.
*Who's there?*
Alice.
*Alice who?*
Alice fair in love and war.

Knock, knock.
*Who's there?*
Hawaii.
*Hawaii who?*
No complaints, how are you?

Knock, knock.
*Who's there?*
Leaf.
*Leaf who?*
Leaf me alone already!

Knock, knock.
*Who's there?*
Iran.
*Iran who?*
Iran all the way here, and now I'm tired.

Knock, knock.
*Who's there?*
To.
*To who?*
It's actually to whom.

Knock, knock.
*Who's there?*
Lettuce.
*Lettuce who?*
Lettuce in, it's freezing!

Knock, knock.
*Who's there?*
Razor.
*Razor who?*
Razor hands, this is a stick up!

Knock, knock.
*Who's there?*
Amarillo.
*Amarillo who?*
Amarillo great guy once you get to know me.

Knock, knock.
*Who's there?*
Candice.
*Candice who?*
Candice conversation go on any longer?

Knock, knock.
*Who's there?*
Boo.
*Boo who?*
I'm sorry, don't cry!

Knock, knock.
*Who's there?*
Cher.
*Cher who?*
Cher would be great of you to open the door.

Knock, knock.
*Who's there?*
Stopwatch.
*Stopwatch who?*
Stopwatch you're doing and open the door!

Knock, knock.
*Who's there?*
Say.
*Say who?*
Okay, who.

Knock, knock.
*Who's there?*
Robin.
*Robin who?*
Robin you! Gimme your candy!

Knock, knock.
*Who's there?*
Voodoo.
*Voodoo who?*
Voodoo you think you're talking to?

Knock, knock.
*Who's there?*
Cash.
*Cash who?*
I prefer peanuts.

Knock, knock.
*Who's there?*
Mustache.
*Mustache who?*
I mustache you a question.

Knock, knock.
*Who's there?*
Alex.
*Alex who?*
Alex plain another time.

Knock, knock.
*Who's there?*
Ketchup.
*Ketchup who?*
Ketchup with me and find out.

Knock, knock.
*Who's there?*
Dishes.
*Dishes who?*
Dishes a nice place you got here!

Knock, knock.
*Who's there?*
Avenue.
*Avenue who?*
Avenue heard me knocking before?

Knock, knock.
*Who's there?*
Viper.
*Viper who?*
Viper runny nose.

Knock, knock.
*Who's there?*
Gerard.
*Gerard who.*
Gerard the way, I'm coming through!

Knock, knock.
*Who's there?*
Justin.
*Justin who?*
Justin time for lunch.

Knock, knock.
*Who's there?*
The interrupting cow.
*The interrupting cow wh-*
MOO!

Knock, knock.
*Who's there?*
Sadie.
*Sadie who?*
Sadie magic words and let me in.

Knock, knock.
*Who's there?*
Abby.
*Abby who?*
Abby birthday to me!

Knock, knock.
*Who's there?*
Isabel.
*Isabel who?*
Isabel not working? Knocking hurts!

Knock, knock.
*Who's there?*
Aida.
*Aida who?*
Aida burger for dinner.

Knock, knock.
*Who's there?*
I am.
*I am who?*
I don't know, who are you?

Knock, knock.
*Who's there?*
Al.
*Al who?*
Al give you a kiss if you open the door!

Knock, knock.
*Who's there?*
Monkey.
*Monkey who?*
Uh, how many monkeys do you know?

Knock, knock.
*Who's there?*
Armageddon.
*Armageddon who?*
Armageddon really bored out here, won't you let me in?

Knock, knock.
*Who's there?*
Annie.
*Annie who?*
Annie thing you can do, I can do better!

Knock, knock.
*Who's there?*
Hal.
*Hal who?*
Hal you know unless you open up the door?

Knock, knock.
*Who's there?*
Nacho.
*Nacho who?*
Nacho problem!

Knock, knock.
*Who's there?*
Woo.
*Woo who?*
I'm excited too!

Knock, knock.
*Who's there?*
Nunya.
*Nunya who?*
Nunya business.

Knock, knock.
*Who's there?*
Beets.
*Beets who?*
Beets me too!

Knock, knock.
*Who's there?*
Butter.
*Butter who?*
Butter open this door quickly, I need to go to the bathroom!

Knock, knock.
*Who's there?*
Donut.
*Donut who?*
Donut ask, it's top secret!

Knock, knock.
*Who's there?*
Alfie.
*Alfie who?*
Alie awful if you don't let me in.

Knock, knock.
*Who's there?*
Barbara.
*Barbara who?*
Barbara black sheep, have you any wool?

Knock, knock.
*Who's there?*
Anyu.
*Anyu who?*
Anyu listen to any more knock-knock jokes?

Knock, knock.
*Who's there?*
Doris.
*Doris who?*
The Doris locked, and I can't find my keys.

Knock, knock.
*Who's there?*
Frank.
*Frank who?*
Franks for always answering the door for me.

Knock, knock.
*Who's there?*
Howard.
*Howard who?*
Howard I know?

Knock, knock.
*Who's there?*
Justin.
*Justin who?*
Justin the neighborhood, though I'd say hello.

Knock, knock.
*Who's there?*
Ken.
*Ken who?*
Ken you let me in? I'm getting really tired of knocking.

Knock, knock.
*Who's there?*
Remy.
*Remy who?*
Remy in and find out.

Knock, knock.
*Who's there?*
Mikey.
*Mikey who?*
Mikey is nowhere to be found, let me in!

Knock, knock.
*Who's there?*
Troy.
*Troy who?*
Troy opening the door, maybe you'll find out.

Knock, knock.
*Who's there?*
A herd.
*A herd who?*
A herd you were at home, won't you let me in?

Knock, knock.
*Who's there?*
Chick.
*Chick who?*
Chick your kitchen, I think I smell something burning!

Knock, knock.
*Who's there?*
The interrupting sloth.
*The interrupting sloth who?*
Slooooooooooth!

Knock, knock.
*Who's there?*
Owls say.
*Owls say who?*
They sure do!

Knock, knock.
*Who's there?*
Some bunny.
*Some bunny who?*
Some bunny better let me in right now!

Knock, knock.
*Who's there?*
Havana.
*Havana who?*
Havana great time out here, but I wish I was in there.

Knock, knock.
*Who's there?*
Ida.
*Ida who?*
It's pronounced Idaho.

Knock, knock.
*Who's there?*
Amish.
*Amish who?*
Amish you too, now let me in!

Knock, knock.
*Who's there?*
Atch.
*Atch who?*
Bless you!

Knock, knock.
*Who's there?*
Bed.
*Bed who?*
Bed you won't be able to guess who I am.

Knock, knock.
*Who's there?*
Broken pencil.
*Broken pencil who?*
Nevermind, this joke is pointless!

Knock, knock.
*Who's there?*
Burglar.
*Burglar who?*
Burglar's don't knock!

Knock, knock.
*Who's there?*
Comb.
*Comb who?*
Comb and open the door!

Knock, knock.
*Who's there?*
Doctor.
*Doctor who?*
I love that TV show!

Knock, knock.
*Who's there?*
Dozen.
*Dozen who?*
Dozen anybody want to open the door?

Knock, knock.
*Who's there?*
Wooden.
*Wooden who?*
Wooden you mind letting me inside?


Knock, knock.
*Who's there?*
Radio.
*Radio who?*
Radio not, I'm coming in!


Knock, knock.
*Who's there?*
Water.
*Water who?*
Water you doing. Let me in already!


Knock, knock.
*Who's there?*
Witches.
*Witches who?*
Witches the quickest way to the store?


Knock, knock.
*Who's there?*
Zoo.
*Zoo who?*
Zoo do you think it is?


Knock, knock.
*Who's there?*
Lena.
*Lena who?*
Lena little closer, and you might find out.

Knock, knock.
*Who's there?*
Quiche.
*Quiche who?*
Wanna give me a hug and a quiche?

Knock, knock.
*Who's there?*
Olive.
*Olive who?*
Olive in the house next door. Just wanted to come say hi!

Knock, knock.
*Who's there?*
June.
*June who?*
June you know how long I've been standing out here?

Knock, knock.
*Who's there?*
Day shaw?
*Day shaw who?*
Knock knock.

Knock, knock.
*Who's there?*
Cargo.
*Cargo who?*
Cargo vroom, vroom, beep, beep!

Knock, knock.
*Who's there?*
Ya.
*Ya who?*
I prefer to use Google.

Knock, knock.
*Who's there?*
Control freak.
*Contr-*
Okay, now you say "control freak who?"

Knock, knock.
*Who's there?*
   Billy Joe Bob Penny.
*Billy Joe Bob Penny who?*
   Do you really know more than one Billy Joe Bob Penny?

Knock, knock.
*Who's there?*
Theodore.
*Thedore who?*
Theodore was closed, so I decided to knock.

Knock, knock.
*Who's there?*
   Alec.
*Alec who?*
   Alec it when you ask me questions.

Knock, knock.
*Who's there?*
Cereal.
*Cereal who?*
Cereal pleasure to be your friend!

Knock, knock.
*Who's there?*
   Cantaloupe.
*Cantaloupe who?*
   Cantaloupe now, you're so young!

Knock, knock.
*Who's there?*
Kenya.
*Kenya who?*
Kenya feel the love tonight?

Knock, knock.
*Who's there?*
Boo.
*Boo who?*
Oh no, why are you crying?

Knock, knock.
*Who's there?*
Time.
*Time who?*
Time waits for no man. No man but me!

Knock, knock.
*Who's there?*
Says.
*Says who?*
Say me, that's who!

Knock, knock.
*Who's there?*
Doctor.
*Doctor who?*
No, just a regular doctor.

Knock, knock.
*Who's there?*
Figs.
*Figs who?*
Figs your doorbell, I hate knocking!

Knock, knock.

*Who's there?*

Amos.

*Amos who?*

Agh, the amos-quito out here! Let me in!

Knock, knock.

*Who's there?*

Thesis.

*Thesis who?*

Thesis the last straw. Open up!

Knock, knock.

*Who's there?*

A Mayan.

*A Mayan who?*

A Mayan the way?

Knock, knock.

*Who's there?*

Abe.

*Abe who?*

Abe, C, D, E!

Knock, knock.

*Who's there?*

Icing.

*Icing who?*

Icing really loudly, can you hear me?

Knock, knock.

*Who's there?*

Nicholas.

*Nicholas who?*

A Nicholas really isn't that much money these days.

Knock, knock.
*Who's there?*
Gorilla.
*Gorilla who?*
Gorilla me a burger, please!

Knock, knock.
*Who's there?*
Kanga.
*Kanga who?*
It's Kangaroo, actually.

Knock, knock.
*Who's there?*
Cabbage.
*Cabbage who?*
You think a cabbage is going to have a last name?

Knock, knock.
*Who's there?*
Sweden.
*Sweden who?*
Sweden sour chicken is my favorite!

# Longer Jokes

## The Dog Ate My Homework

"Where's your homework?" The teacher asked Johnny, looking stern and holding her hand out.

"My dog ate it, miss." Said Johnny, sadly.

"Johnny, I've been teaching for 20 years. You think I'm going to believe that one?"

"It's true, Miss! I swear! I coated it in peanut butter, and he ate the whole thing!"

## The Penguin Field Trip

A bus driver was driving his normal route when he saw a truck from the zoo parked on the side of the road. The zoo worker that was driving the truck offered the bus driver $50 to help him deliver 24 penguins.

The bus driver agreed and loaded the penguins onto his bus. One hour later, the zoo worker got his truck working and drove to the zoo. While he was driving, he saw the bus driver, with the penguins in his bus, driving in the opposite direction that the zoo was.

He caught up to the bus driver, and they both stopped. The zoo worker yelled, "I gave you $50 to bring the penguins to the zoo! Why are you still driving with them?"

"Calm down", said the bus driver. "I took the penguins to the zoo. We still have some change left, so I'm taking them to the movies."

## Chickens in the Library

Two chickens go to the circulation desk at a library, and they say, "Buck, buck, buckaw!" The librarian decided that the chickens wanted three books, so she gave them three books. The chickens left shortly after.

That afternoon, the pair of chickens came back to the desk, looked pretty annoyed. "Buck, buck, BUCKAW!" they said. Once again, the librarian decided that the chickens wanted three more books, so she gave them three more books. Once again, the chickens left.

Later in the afternoon, they return, saying, "Buck BUCKAW!". They looked very annoyed.

The librarian is starting to get a bit suspicious of the chickens now. She gave them what they wanted and then followed them. She followed them out of the library, out of town, and to a park. At this point, she hid behind a tree, trying her hardest not to be seen.

She saw the chickens throwing the books to a frog in a pond, who was saying, "Rrreddit... Rrreddit... Rrreddit..."

## The Three Little Pigs

Three little pigs decided to go out for dinner one night. The waitron came and took their drinks order. The first little pig said, "I want a Sprite, please." The second little pig said, "I want a Coke, please." The third little pig said, "I want water, please. Lots and lots of water."

When their drinks were brought, the waitron took their order for dinner. The first little pig said, "I want a big, juicy steak, please." The second little pig said, "I want a plate of salad, please." The third little pig said, "I want water, please. Lots and lots of water."

The waitron brought the meals out, and after they were finished eating, the waitron came and took their dessert orders. The first little pig said, "I want a banana split sundae, please." The second little pig said, "I want a soda float, please." The third little pig exclaimed, "I want water! Lots and lots of water!"

"Excuse me for asking," the waitron said, "but why do you only order water?" The third little pig said, "Well, someone has to go 'Wee, wee, wee, all the way home!'"

## Animal Football

One day, the animals got very bored. After being bored for so long, the lion finally got an idea. "I know a really exciting game we can play. The humans call it 'football'. I've seen it on their TVs." He described football to the rest of the animals, and they all got so excited, they wanted to play right away.

They went to the field, split into two teams, and were ready to start. The lion's team was the receiver. They got two downs, then had to punt. The donkey punted, and the rhino was back deep for the kick. He caught the ball, put his head down, and charged.

First, he pushed past two rabbits, then a roadrunner. He charged into a cow, then scored six. Unfortunately, they didn't have a placekicker, and the score stayed at 6 - 0. The lion's team scored a touchdown late in the first half, and the donkey kicked the extra point.

At halftime, the lion's team led with 7 - 6. The lion gave his team a pep-talk in the locker room. "We can win this game," he said. "We have the lead, and their only real threat is the rhino. We must keep the ball away from him. Donkey, when you kick off, make sure you stay away from the rhino."

The second half started. Right before the donkey kicked off, the rhino's team changed their formation, and the ball landed right in front of the rhino. Once again, he put his head down and charged. He pushed through two gazelles, then a zebra, then even charged an elephant out of the way.

At the 20 yard line, he suddenly dropped over. He was asleep. There were no other animals near him, except a small centipede. "Did you do this?" the lion asked the centipede. The centipede confirmed that he did. The lion asked, "Where were you in the first half?"

"I was putting on my shoes." replied the centipede.

## The Punchline

A guy asks a girl to prom. She agrees, and he decides that he's going to rent a suit. There's a long line at the rental store, so he has to wait a long time before he can get his suit.

He also decides to buy the girl a bouquet of flowers, so he goes to the florist. There's a long like there as well, so he has to wait quite a while before he can get his bouquet.

He picks the girl up from her home, and they go to the dance. There's a very long line to the prom hall, so they have to wait a while before they can get in.

They finally get into the hall, and the guy offers to get the girl something to drink. She wants punch, so he goes to the drink table to get her some. There's no punch line.

## The Three Friends

Three friends are stranded on an island that is deserted. They find a magic lamp, and inside it, there's a genie who says that he'll grant each friend one wish.

"I wish to go home," says the first friend. The genie grants his wish, and the first friend disappears.

"I wish to go home, too," says the second friend. The genie grants her wish, and the second friend disappears.

"I'm lonely," says the third friend. "I sure wish my friends were here."

## The Sick Chihuahua

A gentleman takes his sick Chihuahua to the vet. They are taken to the backroom immediately.

Shortly after, a Labrador walks in, sniffs at the Chihuahua for five minutes, then leaves. A cat comes in after, stares at the Chihuahua for five minutes, then leaves.

The doctor comes in, hands the owner a prescription for medicine, and gives him a bill for $300.

"There has to be some kind of mistake!" the man says. "We've only been here for ten minutes!"

"There's no mistake," says the doctor. "It's $100 for the lab test, $100 for the cat scan, and $100 for the medicine."

## The Handyman

A businessman went into his office, and there he found an amateur handyman painting the walls. The handyman wore two heavy parkas, even though it was a humid summer's day.

The businessman thought that this was a bit strange, and asked the handyman why he was wearing the parkas when it was so hot outside.

The handyman showed the businessman the instructions that were on the can of paint. They read: "For best results, put on two coats."

## The Prince and the Lady

A prince was put under a spell which only allowed him to speak one word every year. If he didn't speak at all for two years, the next year, he would be able to speak two words, and so on.

One day, he fell in love with a beautiful lady. He did not speak for two years, just so that he could call her "my darling." But he also wanted to tell her that he loved her, so he did not speak for another three years. After the five years had passed, he wanted to ask her to marry him. He waited another four years.

Finally, he had stayed silent for nine years. He took his lady to the most romantic place in the entire kingdom, and when they arrived, he exclaimed, "My darling, I love you! Will you marry me?"

In response, the lady said, "Pardon?"

## The Lady and the Train

A lady takes a seat on a train. There is a man sitting next to her. He turns to her and says, "Lady, that is the ugliest baby I have ever seen. If that baby looks in a mirror, it will shatter. You should put a bag on his head; he's just ugly!"

The horrified woman stands up and calls for the conductor. "Conductor! This man has insulted me."

"I am so sorry, madam," the conductor says. "What he did was completely unacceptable on this train. I will deal with him later, but you can come with me for now. We'll give you a nice, first-class seat - and a banana for your monkey."

# Funny Riddles

**What type of cheese is made backward?**
Edam.

**Why are ghosts bad at lying?**
You can see right through them.

**Imagine you are in a room that is quickly filling with water. There are no doors, nor are there any windows. How do you escape?**
Stop imagining!

**What are the two things that you can never eat for breakfast?**
Lunch and dinner.

**Why do bees hum?**
They never know the words.

**If you threw a blue stone into the Red Sea, what would it become?**
Wet.

**Why did Mickey Mouse go to Outer Space?**
He wanted to visit Pluto.

**What did the beach say when the tide came in?**
Long time, no sea.

**You can serve it, but it can't be eaten. What is it?**
A tennis ball.

**What can you catch but can't throw?**
A cold.

**What goes up and down, yet never moves at all?**
The temperature.

**What starts with 'P', ends with 'E', and has thousands of letters?**
The post office.

**I have wings and a tail. I sail across the sky, yet I have no mouth, eyes, or ears. I bob randomly from north to south. What am I?**
A kite.

**Mr. Blue lives in the Blue House, Ms. Green lives in the Green House, and Mr. Black lives in the Black house. Who lives in the White House?**
The president.

**In a pink house with one story, there lived a pink woman. She had a pink fish, a pink cat, a pink chair, a pink computer, a pink telephone, a pink table, and a pink tower. Everything in her house was pink! What color are her stairs?**
No color at all. She lives in a one-story house!

**What has hands that constantly move, but can't clap?**
A clock.

**What gets wetter and wetter the more it dries?**
A towel.

**You draw a line, and, without touching it, you have to make it longer. How?**
You draw a shorter line next to it, and it becomes the longer line.

**You're walking next to a river, and you see a boat full of people float past. However, there isn't a single person on board. How is this possible?**
Everyone on the boat is married.

**I have no doors, yet I have keys. I have no rooms, yet I have space. You are never able to leave, yet I allow you to enter. What am I?**
A keyboard.

**You have a three-gallon bucket and a five-gallon bucket, and as much water as you need, but no other tools for measuring. How do you fill the five-gallon bucket with exactly four gallons of water?**
Fill the five-gallon bucket entirely. Pour it into the three-gallon bucket until it's full. Empty the three-gallon bucket. Pour the last two gallons (in the five-gallon bucket) into the three-gallon bucket. Fill the five gallon-bucket all the way up, then fill the three-gallon bucket up the rest of the way using the five-gallon bucket. There will be four gallons of water left in the five-gallon bucket.

**They come out at night, but are never called. They disappear in the day, but are never stolen. What are they?**
The stars.

**I have a horn, and I give milk, but I am not a cow. What am I?**
A milk truck.

**What has a mouth but never talks, can run but never walks, has a bed but never sleeps, and has a head but never weeps?**
A river.

**What has a neck, but no head, and wears a cap?**
   A bottle.

**What is so delicate, that even saying its name breaks it?**
   Silence.

**Dorothy's mother has three daughters. One is named Mary, the other is named Sue. What is the third daughter's name?**
   Dorothy!

**What is often answered, but never asks any questions?**
   A doorbell.

**What goes up, but can never come back down?**
   Your age.

**What goes up and down, yet never moves at all?**
   A flight of stairs.

# Ridiculous Facts

1. Giant Pandas eat about 28 pounds of bamboo every day. That's more than 5 tons each year!

2. The Nobel Peace Prize was named after Alfred Nobel, the same man that invented dynamite.

3. Cats cannot taste anything that is sweet. That explains why they're always so bitter!

4. You fart an average of 14 times every day. Each one travels at 7mph.

5. Peanuts are an ingredient used to make dynamite.

6. Kangaroos cannot walk backward.

7. There's a pill that makes your bowel movements smell like chocolate!

8. The shortest war in history lasted for 38 minutes.

9. Sea lions understand rhythm and are the only animal that is able to clap to a beat.

10. You can't smell anything while you are asleep. Not even the most potent of smells.

11. Some tumors grow teeth, hair, fingernails, and even bones.

12. Your brain does not feel pain and uses 10 watts of energy to think.

13. Glass balls are able to bounce higher than balls made of rubber.

14. The Vatican City is the smallest country in the world, taking up only 0.2 square miles.

15. Milk from a hippo is pink!

16. When you are cold, your fingernails grow faster.

17. Snails take the longest naps of any animal, with some lasting up to three years.

18. Most people spend about two weeks of their life waiting at traffic lights.

19. Parents were able to mail their children to their Grandparent's house through the postal service until 1913!

20. If you don't like mosquitoes, consider getting a pet bat. They can eat 3 000 insects in one night.

21. An average cough moves at 60mph, while a sneeze frequently reaches speeds greater than 100mph.

22. There are species of fish that cough. Just like us.

23. Anatidaephobia is the irrational fear that a duck is constantly watching you. Quack!

24. The pupils in a goat's eyes are rectangular.

25. One year is made up of 31 556 926 seconds.

26. Regular soda cans will sink in water, while diet soda cans will float. They're lighter!

27. Birds need gravity to be able to swallow and would not be able to live in space.

28. On an average day, your feet produce one pint of sweat.

29. On Venus, it snows metal.

30. Many mammals, including dogs and cats, walk on their toes, rather than humans, who walk on the soles of their feet.

31. Your brain uses 20% of all the oxygen you breathe.

32. It only takes three cuts to divide a pie into eight pieces.

33. If a zebra and a donkey have a baby, that baby is called a Zonkey.

34. The town with the name that is the most difficult to pronounce is in Wales. It's called Llanfairpwllgwyngyllgogerychwyrndrobwyllllantysiliogogogoch. No, we didn't just make that up.

35. In a group of 23 people, there is a 50% chance that two will share a birthday. In a group of 367 people, it's guaranteed that two will share a birthday. However, you only need a group of 70 people for there to be a 99.9% chance.

36. All babies are born with blue eyes.

37. Have you ever looked at the clear sky and seen some floating, white dots? Those are your white blood cells - you're looking at your own blood.

38. Cows are able to walk up stairs, but not down them.

39. The embryos of a Tiger Shark attack one another in the womb of their mother before she even gives birth.

40. Mars' surface is covered in rust, which is why the planet appears red.

41. It is impossible for a crocodile to stick its tongue out.

42. The heart of a shrimp is in its head.

43. Pigs are physically unable to look up at the sky.

44. You can fracture (break) a rib if you sneeze too hard.

45. Everyone has a unique tongue print, just like they do fingerprints.

46. When refrigerated, rubber bands last longer.

47. Sharks are the only known fish that can blink with both of their eyes.

48. The only word in English that ends with the letters 'mt' is 'Dreamt'.

49. Almonds are part of the peach family!

50. There are 32 muscles in each ear of a cat.

51. An ostrich's brain is smaller than its eye.

52. There are 118 ridges around the edge of a dime.

53.Giant squids have the worlds' largest eyes.

54.It takes most people seven minutes to fall asleep.

55.It is illegal to stand within 90 meters of the Queen of England if you are not wearing socks.

56.Speaking of the Queen, did you know that she has two birthdays?

57.Cows and horses sleep standing up.

58.Driving to space would only take about an hour.

59.Hippos can run faster than humans can.

60.Your ears and nose grow for your entire life.

61.Apples float in water!

62.You can't exhale or inhale while talking. Go on, try!

63.Your heart is around the same size as your fist.

64.The skin of a tiger is also striped like its fur.

65.Frogs drink water through their skin.

66.Like humans, monkeys can go bald as they get older.

67.Female toads do not croak.

68.There are fewer grains of sand on earth than there are stars in the night sky.

69. Owls are physically incapable of moving their eyeballs.

70. In the Daintree rainforest in Australia, there is a tree called the 'Idiot Fruit.'

71. Ostriches can run faster than horses, and males can roar like lions!

72. Pineapple is rich with a digestive enzyme called bromelain, which breaks down protein. When you leave a piece of pineapple in your mouth, it's eating you!

73. Humans are the only animals that blush.

74. The feeling of getting lost inside of a mall is called the Gruen transfer.

75. When you're flying in an airplane, you lose up to 30% of your ability to taste food. That's the deal with airplane food.

76. The tree shrew, and humans are the only mammals on Earth to enjoy spicy foods.

77. 'Set' is the word in the English language with the most definitions, with 430 definitions listed in total.

78. Pigeons can tell the difference between a painting by Picasso and one by Monet. Can you?

79. The dot over a lowercase 'j' or 'i' is called a tittle.

80. Chewing gum can improve your concentration, but you shouldn't chew gum at school!

81. The longest wedding veil in the world was the same length as 63 ½ football fields.

82. The total weight of people on Earth was once the same total weight as ants on the planet.

83. 'E' is the most common letter, and appears in 11% of all words in the English language.

84. An Egyptian pharaoh once coated his slaves in honey in order to keep bees away from him.

85. Depending on its temperature, water makes different sounds when it's poured.

86. Dogs are actually able to understand some words of English. Think about that next time you're talking to your furry friend.

87. Humans are only one of the estimated 8.7 million species of creatures that are present on Earth.

88. If you ever need to pass a kidney stone, riding a rollercoaster might help.

89. Bee Hummingbirds are so small that they often get mistaken for insects.

90. The author of the book 'Dracula' has never even been to Transylvania.

91. Napoleon Bonaparte, the infamous French general, was once attacked by thousands of rabbits.

92. Pigs are protected under the constitution in Florida and have the right to freedom of speech, privacy, and the right for pregnant pigs to be free from cages.

93. The Bermuda Triangle is not more likely to cause mysterious disappearances than any other place on the planet, contrary to popular belief.

94. You can sneeze faster than a cheetah can run.

95. Sharks kill fewer Americans each year than cows do.

96. Your liver is able to regrow itself after three weeks.

97. A 70-year-old woman once completed seven marathons in seven days, in all seven of the continents.

98. Crows hold grudges. Don't get on their bad side! They'll remember you for life.

99. America's first bank robber deposited money into the very same bank that he robbed.

# Funny Tongue Twisters

1. If a blue bug bleeds blue blood, what color blood does a black bug bleed?

2. Any noise annoys an oyster, but a noisy noise annoys an oyster more.

3. Rory's lawn rake really rarely rakes right.

4. If three witches watch three watches, which witch would watch which watch?

5. If you notice a notice, then you notice that the notice is worth noticing.

6. Sarah sold six shoddy sheared sheep on a ship.

7. Betty bought a bit of butter to make the bitter butter better.

8. Does the sports shop stock short socks with spots?

9. Many mumbling merrymakers make merry music in the moonlight.

10. No need to light a night-light on a light night like tonight.

11. Imagine an imaginary menagerie manager managing an imaginary menagerie.

12. Kind kittens knitting mittens keep knitting in the kitten kitchen.

13. A skunk on a stump thunk the stump stunk, and the stump thunk the skunk stunk.

14. Lesser leather doesn't weather wetter weather better than greater leather.

15. I saw a saw that could saw away all other saws I saw.

16. A sailor went to sea to see all he could see, but all he could see was sea, sea, sea.

17. A big bug bit a little beetle, and the little beetle bit the big bug back.

18. Fuzzy Wuzzy is a bear, Fuzzy Wuzzy has no hair. Fuzzy Wuzzy wasn't really fuzzy, was he?

19. Twelve twins twirled twelve twigs while the twigs twist in the twelve twins' hands.

20. The great Greek grape grower grew great Greek grapes.

21. If a dog chews shoes, how does he choose the shoes to chew?

22. Samuel works in a shoeshine shop, where he shines he sits, and where he sits, he shines.

23. Many anemone sees enemy anemone in the sea.

24. How can a clam cram in a clean cream can?

25. Something in a thirty-acre thicket of thermal thistles and thorns thundered and thumped, threatening the 3D thoughts of the thug. Although, thankfully, it was only the thirteen-thousands thorns and thistles through the underneath of his thigh that the thirty-year-old thug thought of then.

26. Can a can can a can as another canner can?

27. I wish to wish the wish you would wish, but if you wish the wish the wizard wishes, I will not wish the wish you wish to wish.

28. There are a thousand thinkers that think that the three thieves went through the thicket.

29. When you write a copy, you own the right to copyright the copy that you write.

30. Bobby Bibby bought a ball. Bobby Bibby bought a bat. With the bat, Bobby banged the ball. Bobby banged it on the wall. Boldly Bobby banged it, that he burst the rubber ball. "Boo!" Bobby cried. Bad luck, ball. Bad luck, Bobby, bad luck ball.

31. I thought of thanking you, now the thought of me thanking you is thought, and you are thanked, I think.

32. Excited executioners exercise their excising powers excessively, excitedly.

33. The big brown bear bit a big brown bug, the big brown bug bit a big black bug. The big black bit the big brown bear, and the big brown bear bit the big bitten black bug again.

34. A tree toad loved a he-toad, who lived in a tree. The he-toad had three toes, but the tree toad had two toes. The three-toed tree toad tried to win

the he-toad's heart, for the tree toad loved the ground that the he-toad trod.

35. The owner of the outside inn was inside the outside inn with is outsides inside the outside inn.

36. Love is a feeling you feel when you are going to feel the feeling that you've never felt before.

37. An optimistic octopus lives inside an octagon, but a pessimistic pest exists amidst us.

38. Shut up the shutters a sternly sit in the shoeshine shop.

39. There was a minimum of cinnamon in the ambient pan.

40. If practice makes perfect, and for perfect, you must practice, then I'm perfectly practiced, and practically perfect!

# Conclusion

Congratulations, kid! You've just made it through the funniest book that this world has ever seen, and you did it without dying from laughter. You're now ready to go out there and have all of your friends and family rolling on the floor laughing.

Try to see how many of these jokes you can memorize. And remember to come back to this book at any time if you're looking for a good laugh!

Printed in Great Britain
by Amazon

68626859R00043